The Nation

Will The U.S. Go To War With Iraq?

STARTING YOUNG: A young member of Saddam's Cubs stands near a portrait of Iraqi leader Saddam Hussein while attending a summer military camp.

The debate over what to do about a dictator who may have dangerous weapons

Either you stop him or we will. That was the message that President George W. Bush brought to the United Nations concerning Iraq's leader, Saddam Hussein. President Bush made his case against

President Bush made his speech amid concerns that the U.S. was ready to move against Iraq—with or without the support of the UN or most U.S. allies. Great Britain has pledged to back the U.S. in any

the time to put strict demands on Hussein—and take action if he does not meet them—is now. They argue that in a post-September 11 world, it's better to be safe than sorry.

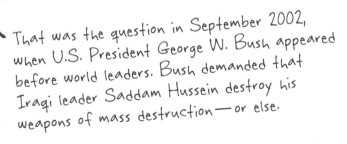

That was the question in September 2002, when U.S. President George W. Bush appeared before world leaders. Bush demanded that Iraqi leader Saddam Hussein destroy his weapons of mass destruction—or else.

So what happened?

The Iraq War began six months later, on March 19, 2003.

COVER STORY

AMERICA ATTACKS

THE U.S. LEADS
A MULTINATIONAL
COALITION IN A
WAR AGAINST IRAQ.

A U.S.-led military force has attacked Iraq in an effort to disarm the country and remove its President, Saddam Hussein, from power.

Since then, about 150,000 Iraqis have died as a result of the war. Four million have become refugees. More than 4,000 American soldiers have been killed.

Why did the war begin? Why have troops been there for so long? Read on to follow the war in Iraq as it unfolded — and as Scholastic's magazines reported it.

Book design: Red Herring Design/NYC

Library of Congress Cataloging-in-Publication Data
The war in Iraq : from the front lines to the home front.
p. cm. - (24/7: behind the headlines)
Includes bibliographical references and index.
ISBN-13: 978-0-531-21807-5 (lib. bdg.)   978-0-531-22003-0 (pbk.)
ISBN-10: 0-531-21807-4 (lib. bdg.)   0-531-22003-6 (pbk.)
1. Iraq War, 2003—Juvenile literature.
DS79.763.W37 2008
956.7044'3–dc22   2008028082

THE
WAR
IN
IRAQ

From the Front Lines
to the Home Front

Franklin Watts®
An Imprint of Scholastic Inc.

CONTENTS

Here's a briefing about the who, what, when, where, and why of the Iraq War.

الله اكبر

THE HEADLINES

Experts estimated that the war would last only a few months. So what happened?

10 2002–2003: THE WAR BEGINS

U.S. President George W. Bush challenges Iraqi dictator Saddam Hussein . . . Says Hussein is a threat to world peace . . . U.S.-led coalition invades Iraq . . .

38 2004 AND BEYOND: NO END IN SIGHT

Hussein toppled . . . War continues . . . Iraqis struggle to rebuild . . . U.S. troops redeployed . . .

THE WAR IN IRAQ:
FAQs

Here's a quick look at the key facts about the Iraq War.

WHERE IS IRAQ?

It's a country in the Middle East. Iraq is bordered by the countries of Saudi Arabia, Jordan, Syria, Turkey, and Iran. It also has a port on the Persian Gulf.

WHEN DID THE IRAQ WAR START?

It started in March 2003, when the U.S. and its allies bombed Baghdad, the capital of Iraq.

WHO WERE THE LEADERS OF THE U.S. AND IRAQ WHEN THE WAR STARTED?

George W. Bush was president of the United States, and Saddam Hussein was dictator of Iraq.

WHY DID THE WAR START?
President Bush and U.S. allies said that Saddam Hussein refused to destroy his dangerous chemical and biological weapons. They also accused him of supporting terrorists.

WHAT WAS THE STRATEGY OF THE U.S. AND ITS ALLIES?
Military officials described the strategy as "shock and awe." The plan was for a coalition of the U.S. and its allies to scare Iraqi troops into surrendering by bombing Iraq and then sending in troops.

DID THIS STRATEGY WORK?
At first, yes. The U.S.-led coalition took Baghdad very quickly. But no chemical or biological weapons were found. The fighting continued as various religious and political groups battled the U.S. and each other.

WHAT HAPPENED AFTER THE INVASION?
The fighting got worse. A democratic government was formed, but daily violence made life hard. By 2008, an estimated 150,000 Iraqis had died as a result of the war. Millions had become refugees. U.S. casualties numbered more than 4,000 killed and 30,000 wounded. But there were also signs of progress: violence was down, and the political situation was improving.

THE WAR IN IRAQ: FACTS & FIGURES

THE PEOPLE OF IRAQ

Here's a look at the major religious and ethnic groups within Iraq.

RELIGIOUS GROUPS

97% of Iraqis are Muslim—followers of the religion of Islam. Muslims believe that Allah is God, and that Muhammad is Allah's prophet. There are two main branches of Islam:

SHIITES: Most Iraqi Muslims are Shiite. They were oppressed under Saddam Hussein. Today, Shiites dominate the Iraqi government.

SUNNIS: Worldwide, most Muslims are Sunni. In Iraq, they are in the minority. Saddam Hussein was a Sunni, and his government was run by Sunnis.

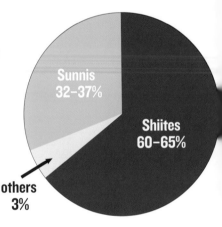

Sunnis
32–37%

Shiites
60–65%

others
3%

ETHNIC GROUPS

ARABS: Most Iraqis are Arabs—descendants of a group of people from the Arabian Peninsula.

KURDS: A non-Arab group made up mostly of Sunni Muslims. There are Kurds in Turkey, Iraq, and several other countries. They were brutally oppressed by Saddam Hussein.

OTHERS: There are also Turkomans, Assyrians, and Chaldeans in Iraq.

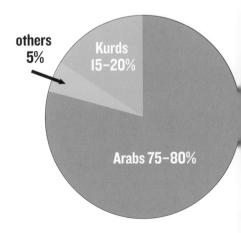

others
5%

Kurds
15–20%

Arabs 75–80%

A DIVIDED COUNTRY

Except in a few areas of the country, Iraq's ethnic and religious groups tend to live in separate regions.

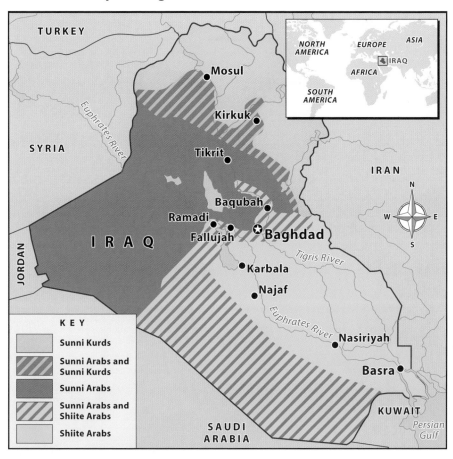

TURKEY

Mosul

Kirkuk

SYRIA

Tikrit

IRAN

Baqubah

Ramadi

I R A Q

Fallujah

Baghdad

JORDAN

Karbala

Najaf

Tigris River

Euphrates River

KEY

- Sunni Kurds
- Sunni Arabs and Sunni Kurds
- Sunni Arabs
- Sunni Arabs and Shiite Arabs
- Shiite Arabs

Nasiriyah

Basra

KUWAIT

SAUDI ARABIA

Persian Gulf

NORTH AMERICA EUROPE ASIA

IRAQ

AFRICA

SOUTH AMERICA

N
W E
S

The flag of Iraq, as of 2008. The writing says *Allahu Akbar*, which means "God is great."

FACTS TO KNOW

AREA: 169,236 square miles (slightly larger than California)

POPULATION: 27,500,000

ECONOMY: Oil dominates the economy, which has been weakened by the war.

LANGUAGE: Mostly Arabic. The Kurds speak Kurdish.

2002–2003

THE WAR BEGINS

**THIS SECTION'S
HEADLINE ARTICLES:**

- ▸ Will the U.S. Go to War?
- ▸ Protesters Call for Peace
- ▸ U.S.-Led Forces Attack Iraq
- ▸ War Diary
- ▸ Baghdad Falls!
- ▸ A Land in Turmoil
- ▸ An Uncertain Future
- ▸ "Caught Like a Rat"

WAR ZONE: U.S. soldiers on patrol in the city
of Ramadi in 2003.

WILL THE U.S. GO TO WAR WITH IRAQ?

President Bush tells Saddam Hussein to give up his weapons—or else.

AT THE UN: President Bush makes his case on September 12, 2002.

Either you stop him or we will. That was the message that U.S. President George W. Bush brought to world leaders about Iraq's leader, Saddam Hussein.

President Bush made his case against Hussein in a speech on September 12, 2002, at the United Nations (UN). The UN is an organization of countries from around the world.

Bush asked the UN to demand that Hussein destroy all of Iraq's weapons of mass destruction (WMDs). WMDs are biological, chemical, or nuclear weapons that can kill large numbers of people or cause massive destruction.

Bush also accused Hussein of supporting terrorists and demanded that he cut his ties to them.

"The just demands of peace and security will be met," the president said, "or action will be unavoidable."

WHY SADDAM HUSSEIN?

This is not the first time the U.S. opposed Saddam Hussein. In August 1990, Hussein's military forces invaded the nearby country of Kuwait and occupied its oil fields. In response, the U.S. and its allies launched the Gulf War to restore Kuwait's independence.

The allies quickly drove Iraq out of Kuwait, but Hussein remained in power. The UN ordered him to destroy all of his

THE GULF WAR: After being defeated in March 1991, Saddam Hussein's retreating forces set fire to hundreds of oil wells in Kuwait. Here, U.S. firefighters approach one of the wells.

13

A SHOW OF FORCE: Iraqi fighters march past a statue of Saddam Hussein in 2000.

WMDs. Hussein was also told to allow weapons inspectors into his country to make sure he obeyed. But in 1998, Hussein stopped cooperating with UN inspectors.

THE TIME TO ACT

At the UN this month, President Bush argued that Hussein is a "grave danger" to world peace.

President Bush and many others still fear that Iraq is hiding WMDs that could be used against the U.S. and other nations. Some people also suspect that Saddam Hussein has ties to the deadly Al Qaeda terrorist network.

"To assume this regime's good faith is to bet the lives of millions of people and the peace of the world in a reckless gamble," President Bush said. "And this is a risk we must not take."

Some world leaders have voiced support for the president's tough stand. Saddam Hussein "has had ten years of second chances," said a member of the British Parliament. "Now surely is the time to act."

But most world leaders—and many U.S. citizens—disagree. "The most important task now," said Russian President Vladimir

Putin, "is the quickest possible return of international inspectors to Iraq."

Many Middle Eastern leaders worry that a war in Iraq would only add to the problems of a region already torn by violence and instability. "We fear a state of disorder and chaos," said Egyptian President Hosni Mubarak.

Despite strained relations, the U.S. relies on Iraq and other Middle Eastern nations for oil. In the first six months of 2002, the U.S. imported 110 million barrels of crude oil from Iraq. An attack on Iraq could jeopardize the United States' access to this oil.

The Bully of Baghdad

For decades, dictator Saddam Hussein has dominated Iraq.

SEPT 2002—Saddam Hussein has been "very cruel and ruined our lives." That's according to a 13-year-old girl living in Hussein's Iraq. "He [has stolen] everything for himself and left us nothing," she says.

Saddam Hussein is a brutal dictator. He has allowed many people to go hungry while he's grown rich. He has killed political opponents and their family members. He has even used chemical weapons against his own people.

Hussein, a Sunni, controls a huge secret police force that has spied on, tortured, and even killed Shiites who oppose him. He has repressed the Kurds, a minority group in northern Iraq. He wants to gain control of their oil-rich region. His soldiers once used poison gas to kill thousands of Kurds.

The Iraqi dictator has also led his country into costly wars. His war against Iran—a Shiite-run country—lasted from 1980 to 1988. A million people died, and the war bankrupted Iraq. Desperate for money, Hussein attacked Kuwait in 1990 to seize its oil fields.

A U.S.-led coalition quickly drove Hussein out of Kuwait, but he remained in power in Iraq.

BRUTAL LEADER: Saddam Hussein has ruled Iraq with an iron fist.

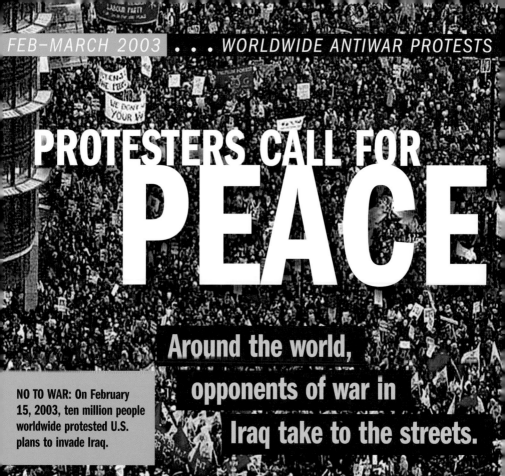

PROTESTERS CALL FOR PEACE

Around the world, opponents of war in Iraq take to the streets.

NO TO WAR: On February 15, 2003, ten million people worldwide protested U.S. plans to invade Iraq.

They were parents, grandparents, teens, and small children. They were military veterans and students—from the U.S., Britain, France, South Africa, and other countries. On February 15, 2003, they marched in more than 600 cities. Their message: "No war on Iraq."

In London, 750,000 people filled the streets. In Berlin, there were an estimated 500,000 protesters.

One million marched in Rome.

In New York City, 100,000 people braved freezing temperatures to make their voices heard. One woman, whose firefighter son was killed in the September 11, 2001 attacks, told CNN that her son was at the World Trade Center "to save lives. I don't feel that he would sanction innocent [blood]—either in this country or in Iraq—being shed in his name."

16

Many protesters carried angry signs aimed at U.S. President George W. Bush. In recent months, the president has put increasing emphasis on military action in Iraq. About 250,000 U.S. troops have been sent to the Gulf region.

After the protests, the president said that he welcomed "people's right to say what they believe." But, he added, "I respectfully disagree" with those who think that Saddam Hussein is not a threat to world peace.

Hussein allowed UN weapons inspectors back into Iraq last November. Kofi Annan, secretary general of the UN, said that was a good sign. President Bush remains skeptical. But he said that war can be prevented if Iraq cooperates fully with the inspectors and destroys weapons that violate UN agreements. "War is my last choice," the president said. "But the risk of doing nothing is even a worse option."

STOCKING UP: A woman in Baghdad heads home with groceries for her family.

THE FINAL HOURS
Iraqis prepare for war.

With the March 19, 2003 deadline for war looming, Iraqis are stocking up on emergency supplies and waiting in long lines to fill their cars with gas. In Baghdad, the price of water doubled overnight and the price of potatoes tripled. Some residents fled, fearing that a U.S. attack would destroy their city.

"We're in the last hour before the war," said Souad Saleh, a housewife. "The mood of war is everywhere. It is all very depressing and sad. We just don't know what to do."

In a television address on March 17, President Bush told U.S. citizens that "events in Iraq have now reached the final days of decision. . . . Peaceful efforts to disarm the Iraqi regime have failed again and again." The president then gave Hussein until 8 P.M. on March 19 to leave Iraq or face war.

17

WAR!

U.S.-LED FORCES ATTACK IRAQ

U.S. and coalition troops invade Iraq.

FIRST STRIKE: A Tomahawk cruise missile is launched from a U.S. warship.

O n Wednesday, March 19, 2003, at 10:15 P.M., U.S. President George W. Bush told the nation that the U.S.-led war against Iraq was under way. About 45 minutes earlier, U.S. forces had launched the first air strikes.

The strikes began shortly after the deadline given by President Bush to Saddam Hussein had passed. On March 17, Bush gave Hussein 48 hours

INTO BATTLE: U.S. sailors on an aircraft carrier in the Persian Gulf rush bombs to waiting fighter jets.

to leave the country or face war. Hussein refused to leave.

In the predawn attack, 40 U.S. Tomahawk cruise missiles exploded in the suburbs south of Baghdad. The missiles were fired from navy ships in the Red Sea and Persian Gulf. They were followed by powerful bombs called bunker busters, fired from air force F-117 stealth fighter jets.

The attack was aimed at what officials hinted might have been a bunker where Saddam Hussein was staying. Hours later, however, Hussein appeared on Iraqi TV and condemned the American attack.

A MASSIVE ATTACK

In his address, President Bush described the strikes as "the opening stages of what will be a broad and concerted campaign." He said that more than 35 nations had joined the U.S. and Great Britain in a coalition to "liberate the Iraqi people."

The initial missile attack quickly turned into a massive bombing campaign and the beginning of fighting on the ground. President Bush said that the road ahead might be difficult, but he insisted that it would be worth it.

"We come to Iraq with respect

TAKING OFF: A U.S. fighter jet sets out on a bombing mission.

for its citizens, for their great civilization, and for the religious faiths they practice," the president said. "We have no ambitions in Iraq, except to remove a threat and restore control of that country to its own people."

Bush promised that the full power of the U.S. military would be used to unseat Saddam Hussein and to disarm Iraq of weapons of mass destruction.

"We will accept no outcome but victory," President Bush said. "We will defend our freedom. We will bring freedom to others. And we will prevail."

TRAINING: British troops prepare for war in the desert of Kuwait.

The Coalition
Who took part in the invasion of Iraq?

MARCH 2003—The invasion of Iraq was backed by a coalition of more than 35 countries. The majority of the combat troops came from the United States (250,000); Great Britain (40,000); and Australia (2,000). Other countries provided support and security for the fighting forces.

Who wasn't part of the coalition? Some longtime U.S. allies such as France and Germany refused to take part in the invasion of Iraq.

The Coalition's Strategy
Step 1: Drops bombs; scare Iraqi troops into surrendering.
Step 2: Send in ground forces to secure the country.

The war began on March 19, when missiles fired from navy ships in the Red Sea and Persian Gulf hit targets near Baghdad.

In the following days, the coalition carried out a "shock and awe" strategy. U.S. forces dropped thousands of satellite-guided "smart" bombs on military targets. Shortly after the initial bombing campaign, troops entered Iraq from neighboring Kuwait.

Some ground troops headed for Basra to secure oil fields in the area. Others headed for Baghdad. Their goals were to disarm Iraq, to overthrow Saddam Hussein's regime, and to install a new government.

THE MIDDLE EAST: SPRING 2003

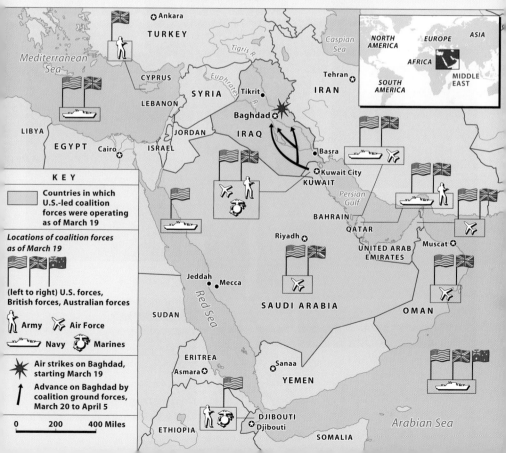

KEY

Countries in which U.S.-led coalition forces were operating as of March 19

Locations of coalition forces as of March 19

(left to right) U.S. forces, British forces, Australian forces

Army　Air Force
Navy　Marines

Air strikes on Baghdad, starting March 19

Advance on Baghdad by coalition ground forces, March 20 to April 5

0　200　400 Miles

Today's Soldier

Here's the gear many U.S. soldiers carried
when they went into battle in Iraq.

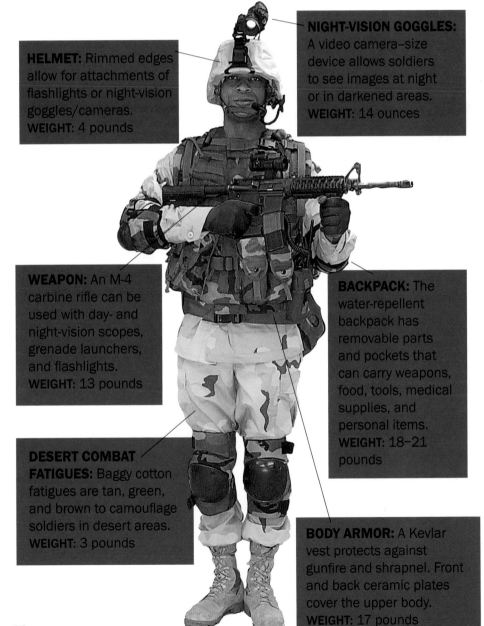

NIGHT-VISION GOGGLES: A video camera–size device allows soldiers to see images at night or in darkened areas. **WEIGHT:** 14 ounces

HELMET: Rimmed edges allow for attachments of flashlights or night-vision goggles/cameras. **WEIGHT:** 4 pounds

WEAPON: An M-4 carbine rifle can be used with day- and night-vision scopes, grenade launchers, and flashlights. **WEIGHT:** 13 pounds

BACKPACK: The water-repellent backpack has removable parts and pockets that can carry weapons, food, tools, medical supplies, and personal items. **WEIGHT:** 18–21 pounds

DESERT COMBAT FATIGUES: Baggy cotton fatigues are tan, green, and brown to camouflage soldiers in desert areas. **WEIGHT:** 3 pounds

BODY ARMOR: A Kevlar vest protects against gunfire and shrapnel. Front and back ceramic plates cover the upper body. **WEIGHT:** 17 pounds

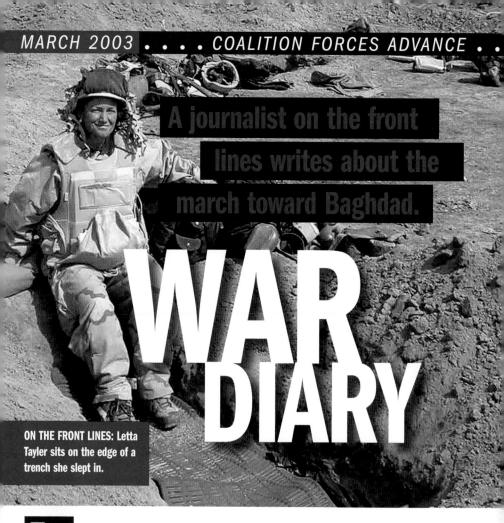

A journalist on the front lines writes about the march toward Baghdad.

WAR DIARY

ON THE FRONT LINES: Letta Tayler sits on the edge of a trench she slept in.

Letta Tayler was one of the hundreds of reporters who covered the invasion of Iraq. She traveled with a U.S. Marines combat unit. Just after the war began on March 19, 2003, Tayler's unit joined a huge force of tanks, armored vehicles, and supply trucks that was moving north to occupy the Iraqi capital of Baghdad.

Here are some excerpts from Tayler's reporting during the first two weeks of the war.

MARCH 21, 2003

Even with their overwhelming military superiority, U.S. ground forces have found the road to Baghdad fraught with pitfalls. They include [hard-to-find] targets, deadly ambushes, blinding sandstorms that slowed the troops to a crawl—and traffic jams.

MARCH 28

I've spent a second night with my Marine unit camped in a

garbage dump. We are surrounded by old cans of oil, rusted car radiators, rotten shoes, filthy rags, and abandoned tires. We literally dig trenches down into this rot and sleep in it.

MARCH 29

Like the soldiers, I eat MREs. [That stands for Meals Ready to Eat. They're instant meals provided by the military.] They come in 24 different flavors—ranging from jambalaya to pasta Alfredo to meat loaf. About the size of a paperback book, they can be heated in 15 minutes by placing them in a bag with water that activates a chemical heating strip.

APRIL 3

The people of a ramshackle village nestled along the banks of the Tigris River greeted U.S. Marines with waves and smiles. Children touched the troops' uniforms with curious, dust-smeared hands. Men in flowing robes offered them sweet tea in small glasses, and women swathed head to toe in black gave them sticky dates wrapped in freshly baked flat bread. Even the woolly sheep came out and gaped.

PALS: Lincoln with a fellow female soldier, PFC Morgan.

DEAR MOM
A young soldier writes home from the front lines.

Brittney Lincoln had just turned 21 when the Iraq War began. She was one of five women in a unit of 60 soldiers. Their job was to take care of Patriot missiles.

Here's a letter she wrote home four days after the war began. She returned safely to Texas in June 2003.

MARCH 24, 2003

It was March 20 at 12:25 **P.M.** That's when the war started for us. Our radar and [electrical equipment] were down. We got word that we had to [get going] anyway, even if our stuff didn't work.

All of a sudden the loudest sound I ever heard came from [a nearby group of soldiers]. We saw a missile fly into the air. Then we realized, "Oh, no!" because it might [be a chemical weapon]. We had to get into our protective gear and wait about two hours for the all clear. Talk about being hot! Sweat was dripping down [our necks].

Finally we left. I drove the truck pulling the missile launcher. It was so dark and the launchers kick up so much dust it was hard to see—but I kept up.

That night I pulled guard duty with one of the guys who thinks it's funny to try to scare me. Believe me, I was scared. The whole sky was lit up with rockets, missiles, and fires in the distance.

We stayed there for two days because of a sandstorm. It was really amazing. I would try to fall backwards and couldn't—that's how strong the wind was.

Did you hear about the maintenance group from the 507th that was attacked? Some of the people killed were my friends. I can't even imagine what their families are going through right now.

On the Home Front
A girl in the U.S. worries about her brother in Iraq.

APRIL 2003—With U.S. troops at war, watching news reports can be especially tense for military families. "Whenever the news is on, and they say another soldier has been killed, I cross my fingers and pray that it wasn't my brother," says Elizabeth Gruchy.

An eighth grader in Quincy, Massachusetts, Elizabeth is waiting for the safe return of her brother Tommy, a lance corporal in the U.S. Marines. Life at home has changed now that Tommy is not around.

WAITING: Elizabeth Gruchy holds a photo of her brother.

"My house is very quiet," Elizabeth says. "He always used to tell jokes and make everyone laugh."

While she waits for Tommy to return, Elizabeth tries to think about happy memories. Each winter, for example, the two would snowboard in their backyard.

What would Elizabeth say to Tommy if she could talk to him now?

"I would tell him that when he is fighting [he should] not give up, and to know that he will be coming home soon."

BAGHDAD FALLS!

U.S.-led forces take control of Iraq's capital city after three weeks of fighting.

Tanks and troops rolled into the center of Baghdad on April 9, 2003, as U.S. forces took control of the capital from Saddam Hussein and his government. Cheering Iraqis took to the streets, tearing down and burning pictures of their former dictator. Scenes of people toppling a large

TOPPLED: U.S. Marines in Baghdad pull down a giant statue of Saddam Hussein.

statue of Saddam Hussein were broadcast around the world.

"Downtown Baghdad is seeing evidence of collapse of any central regime authority," said U.S. Vice President Dick Cheney. "Pockets of resistance remain but are ineffective."

But U.S. officials were hesitant to declare a full victory. "There is still a lot of fighting ahead," warned Cheney. Several cities in northern Iraq are still controlled by Iraqi troops, he said.

U.S. officials declared it to be a "great" and "historic" day for Iraqis and Americans. But they emphasized that there is still much work to do.

The most immediate challenge for U.S. forces is restoring law and order. With the collapse of Saddam Hussein's government, there is no police force. Iraqi citizens also lack electricity, enough medicine and food, and clean water. Lawlessness is on the rise, and Baghdad is plagued by looting.

U.S. Defense Secretary Donald Rumsfeld said he was pleased that U.S. troops had taken Baghdad. But, he added, "We will not stop until Saddam Hussein's regime has been removed from every corner of that country."

Saddam Hussein and his top aides are still at large.

A LAWLESS CITY: Looters haul away stolen goods in broad daylight.

Looting in Baghdad
Chaos allows looters to run wild.

APRIL 2003—After Saddam Hussein's government collapsed, looters took to the streets and ransacked government buildings, libraries, and the dictator's palaces. Looters took whatever they came across— light fixtures, furniture, and industrial equipment. They also stole medical supplies from hospitals.

Even the National Museum of Iraq was looted. It is home to priceless artwork spanning 7,000 years of civilization. Many of the museum's treasures were stolen or destroyed.

The looting terrified many Iraqis. But their fear soon turned to anger—at the looters and at U.S. troops who were not prepared to handle the chaos.

PRISONERS FREED

Captured U.S. troops are found.

It was a joyful and teary reunion. On April 13, 2003, Iraqi soldiers led U.S. Marines to the prison outside Baghdad where seven American prisoners of war (POWs) had been held for 22 days. The POWs—six men and one woman—were alive, although two had been wounded.

"This was probably the most inspiring event of the war so far," said Captain George Benson, whose troops found the POWs. "They were elated."

One of the prisoners was Shoshana Johnson. She suffered bullet wounds to her ankles during the gunfight that led to her capture. Johnson is the first female African American POW in the history of the United States.

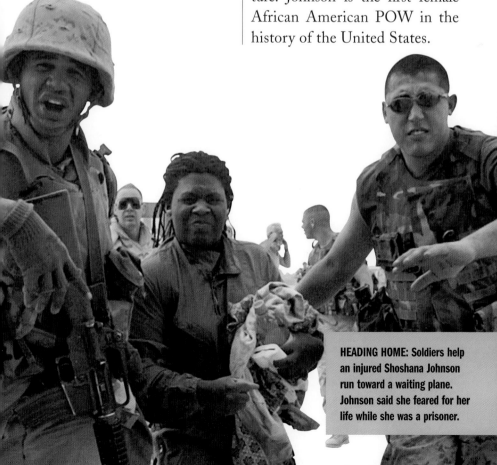

HEADING HOME: Soldiers help an injured Shoshana Johnson run toward a waiting plane. Johnson said she feared for her life while she was a prisoner.

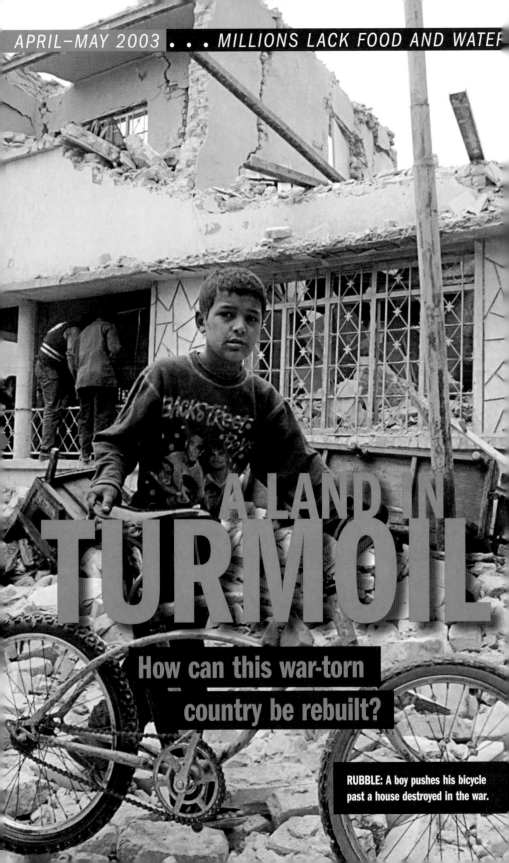

A LAND IN TURMOIL

How can this war-torn country be rebuilt?

RUBBLE: A boy pushes his bicycle past a house destroyed in the war.

IN NEED: Iraqis gather at the back of a truck as boxes of food and water are handed out. Millions of Iraqis lack basic necessities.

In April 2003, not long after Saddam Hussein's statue was pulled down, coalition leaders established an office in one of the dictator's former palaces. There they began a new mission: rebuilding Iraq.

The most pressing need in Iraq is humanitarian aid. As a result of the war, many people are struggling for survival. They don't have enough food, water, and medicine.

One *New York Times* reporter wrote about his encounter with a small Iraqi boy. The boy approached him and said two words over and over: "America. Good." Then he shook his hand and pointed to the sky in a plea for water.

For more than a week, the boy's town, Najaf, was without water. Fierce battles there and elsewhere kept relief organizations from distributing aid.

REMAKING THE GOVERNMENT

The U.S. wants to turn over control of Iraq to the Iraqis themselves, perhaps within the next year. But first a new government must be formed.

Ethnic tensions are a big problem in Iraq. Arabs are the major ethnic group, and the Kurds are a large minority group. The two peoples don't get along.

Iraqis are also divided by religious differences between two branches of Islam—Sunnis and Shiites. There are more Shiites in Iraq than Sunnis. But under Saddam Hussein, Sunnis ran the government, and most were better off than the Shiites.

Saddam Hussein may have been a brutal dictator, but his heavy hand helped control these divisions and hold the country together. It will be a major challenge to bring the various groups together in a new government.

Still, many Shiites and Kurds are happy that they will finally have a say in how their country is run.

"The problem was with Saddam Hussein, not with the Iraqi people," said one Shiite leader who returned from exile when the war began. "We want real democracy."

MISSION ACCOMPLISHED
Bush declares an end to the fighting in Iraq.

"Major combat operations in Iraq have ended," announced U.S. President Bush on May 1, 2003. He was aboard the USS *Abraham Lincoln*, an aircraft carrier. He spoke in front of a banner reading, "Mission Accomplished."

"In the battle of Iraq, the United States and our allies have prevailed. And now our coalition is engaged in securing and reconstructing that country," President Bush said.

"The transition from dictatorship to democracy will take time, but it is worth every effort," the president added. "Our coalition will stay until our work is done. Then we will leave, and we will leave behind a free Iraq."

IT'S OVER: On May 1, 2003, President Bush announced the end of major fighting in Iraq.

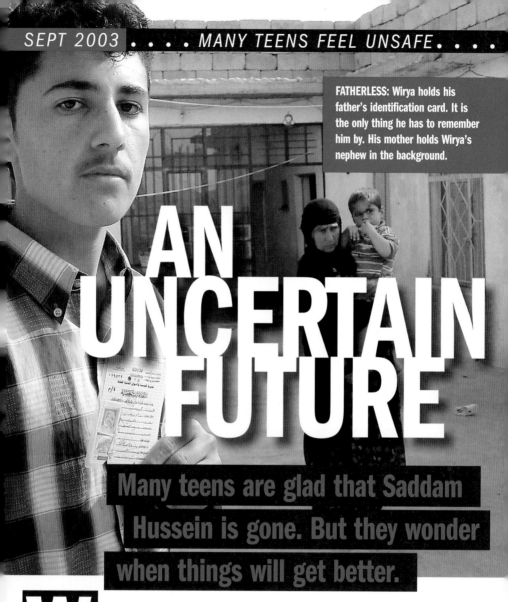

FATHERLESS: Wirya holds his father's identification card. It is the only thing he has to remember him by. His mother holds Wirya's nephew in the background.

AN UNCERTAIN FUTURE

Many teens are glad that Saddam Hussein is gone. But they wonder when things will get better.

Wirya Dizin, 14, was happy to see the U.S.-led coalition topple Saddam Hussein's government. "These days are the happiest of my life," Wirya says.

Wirya is from a Kurdish family originally from Kirkuk, a city in northern Iraq. For years, Iraqi Kurds were victims of Saddam Hussein's cruelty.

In September 1988, when Wirya's mom was pregnant with him, Hussein's soldiers arrested Wirya's father, Kazam. They did it because he was a Kurd. No one ever heard from Kazam again. His family believes he was killed.

33

Several days later, soldiers came to the Dizin home in the middle of the night. They stole the family's possessions and bulldozed their house into ruins.

The family fled to the Binislawa refugee camp in northern Iraq. Wirya was born there, and he still lives at the camp.

The arrest of Wirya's father was part of Saddam Hussein's violent campaign against Kurds in northern Iraq. Between February and September 1988, Saddam ordered Kurdish villages destroyed. He also ordered the use of chemical weapons against Kurds. Some human rights groups estimate that between 50,000 to 100,000 Iraqi Kurds were killed during this time.

"My hope is to return to our land," Wirya says. With Saddam Hussein gone, Wirya's dream just might come true.

FEELING UNSAFE

Yasemin Ehsan, 16, is also happy that U.S.-led forces drove Saddam Hussein from power last spring. Her family suffered greatly under Hussein's dictatorship. Two of her mother's cousins were murdered, and her grandfather was forbidden to leave Baghdad.

Her mother is a member of the Shiite branch of Islam. Under Hussein's Sunni-dominated government, Shiites were killed and imprisoned by the thousands.

Yasemin's middle-class neighborhood in Baghdad has been transformed by the war and its aftermath. Water, gasoline, and electricity are in short supply. And there's violence—attacks against coalition forces and fights between rival militias. People are afraid to go out after dark because looters and other criminals rule the streets.

Yasemin's father, a high school teacher, drives her and her sister, Fatin, 20, to school each day. He is afraid his daughters will be kidnapped.

Despite such concerns,

MOTHERLESS: Namir, 14, has been homeless since his mother was killed in the war. He helps U.S. soldiers in exchange for food and companionship.

NEW LESSONS: Ahmed Walid (center) is glad he no longer has to learn about Hussein's so-called heroic accomplishments.

Yasemin believes that U.S. officials will help make Iraq a better country. But, she adds, Iraqis must be able to determine their own future. "We should have freedom and democracy without anybody forcing us to do anything we don't want to do," she says.

FEAR AND ANGER

Rafid Qalib, 16, is also glad that Saddam Hussein is gone. But he's worried about the future. Rafid says that his father, a military officer, became jobless after Saddam Hussein's government was toppled.

"I have no reason to be happy right now," Rafid says, "even though it's good that Saddam Hussein is gone. We need security on our streets. I don't feel safe."

At Rafid's school, the students sit in crammed classrooms that have no electricity. They sweat in the 100-degree heat. Their textbooks are tattered and torn. Many teens don't even go to school because they're worried about safety. Even teachers are afraid. They receive $20 a month from the U.S. government, but many stay home.

Ahmed Walid, 14, says that one subject he does not miss is patriotism. "It was all about how Saddam Hussein's the greatest," he explains. After the war, Ahmed and his friends playfully drew beards on photos of Hussein in their textbooks.

Yasemin dreams of living in a free and democratic Iraq. But many teens in this war-scarred country just wonder when things will begin to get better.

35

"CAUGHT LIKE A RAT"

Saddam Hussein is captured.

HIDING PLACE: On December 13, 2003, U.S. soldiers removed the cover of this "spider hole" and found Saddam Hussein.

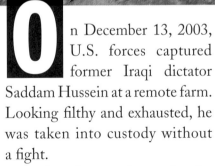

EX-DICTATOR: Hussein shortly after his capture.

On December 13, 2003, U.S. forces captured former Iraqi dictator Saddam Hussein at a remote farm. Looking filthy and exhausted, he was taken into custody without a fight.

U.S. forces learned the location of Hussein's hideout after questioning one of his associates. A force of 600 U.S. soldiers then closed in on two farmhouses near Tikrit, Hussein's ancestral home.

After an intensive search, soldiers discovered a trapdoor that was covered by dirt and a rug. They opened it and found Hussein hiding in an underground hole. "He was caught like a rat," said an army major.

Saddam Hussein had been hiding for months, moving among 20 to 30 hideouts.

Young Iraqis Speak Out

Here's what some young Iraqis had to say after Saddam Hussein was captured.

Dunia, 14: I am glad the Americans captured Saddam. I want the Americans to stay and help stop the [violence], but they should only stay one or two years. They should help teach us how to do things right and then leave.

Noor, 13: Saddam was very cruel and ruined our lives. He stole everything for himself and left us nothing. I am glad the Americans freed us from Saddam, but I think they should leave now. More troops in Iraq would just mean more hardship for Iraqis. It will create chaos without offering us anything in return.

Ahmed, 10: I am very scared about the future of Iraq. Things are more dangerous now than before the war. Saddam was very bad, but most of the time things were peaceful. Now there are explosions and fighting every day.

Gleesan, 10: Saddam Hussein killed my father and held my big brother in prison for five years. My brother was beaten every day. . . . I am now tortured by the memories. My mind is tired and I am tired all of the time. I just want to live quietly.

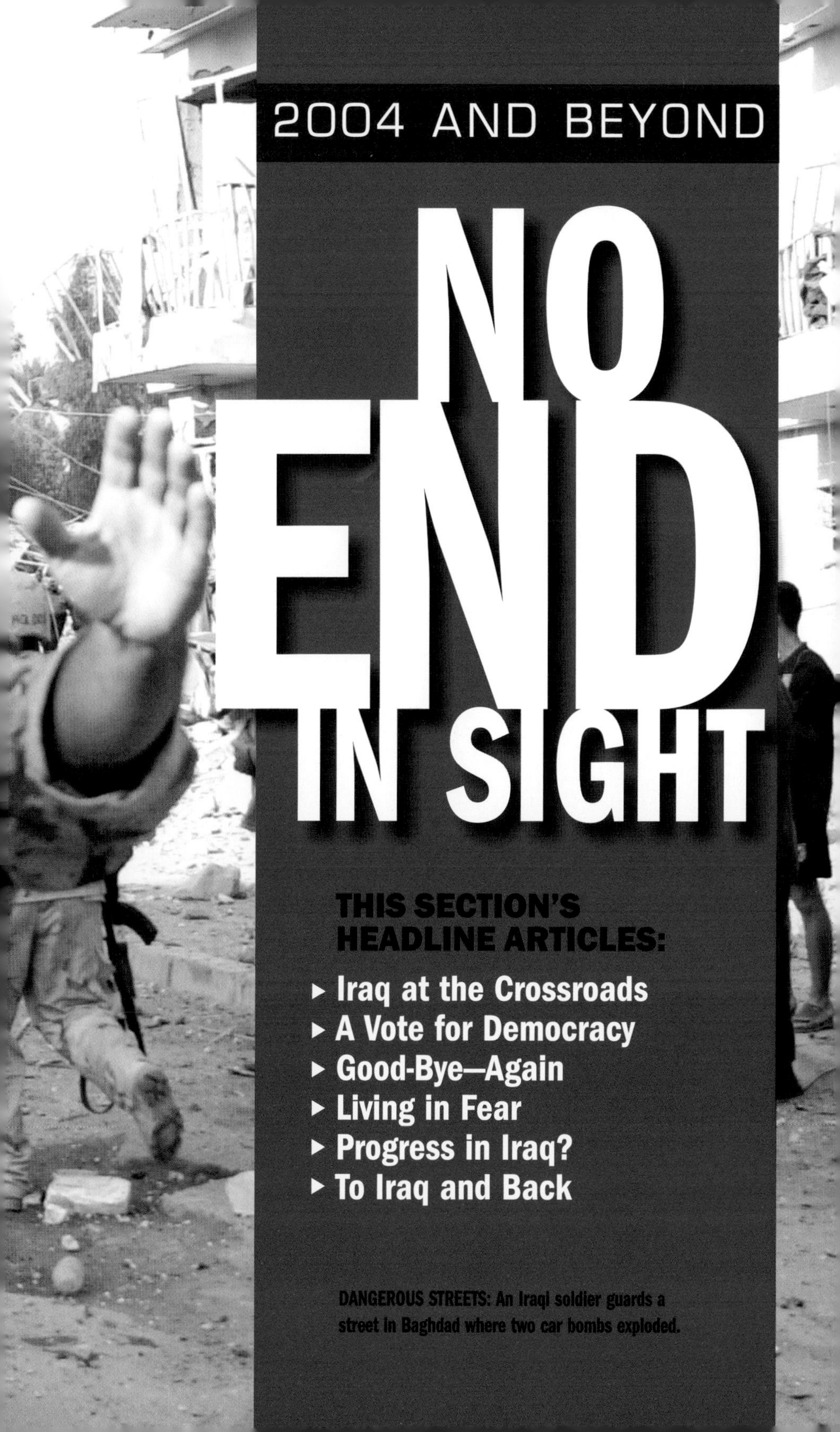

2004 AND BEYOND

NO END IN SIGHT

THIS SECTION'S HEADLINE ARTICLES:

- Iraq at the Crossroads
- A Vote for Democracy
- Good-Bye—Again
- Living in Fear
- Progress in Iraq?
- To Iraq and Back

DANGEROUS STREETS: An Iraqi soldier guards a street in Baghdad where two car bombs exploded.

IRAQ
AT THE CROSSROADS

IN THE LINE OF FIRE: A family stands outside their home. It was hit by a stray rocket when insurgents fired at a U.S. base.

Will there be peace in Iraq—or chaos?

In September 2004, a year and a half after U.S.-led forces toppled Saddam Hussein, Iraq still feels like a country at war. U.S. tanks thunder down Baghdad's streets, where U.S. soldiers still clash with Iraqi insurgents (rebels). Rebels fire rocket-propelled grenades across the Tigris River at the Green Zone. That's a giant concrete-walled compound in central Baghdad that is home to U.S. officials and troops.

40

Most Baghdad neighborhoods get only a few hours of electricity a day. The rest of the time, people cook by candlelight and cool off with "Iraqi air conditioners"— little straw fans. At night, many Iraqis seek relief from the heat by sleeping on their rooftops. Long lines for gasoline and food are common. And sometimes there's no water.

Since the coalition invaded Iraq in March 2003, no weapons of mass destruction have been found. And no connection between Iraq and Al Qaeda, the terrorist group responsible for the September 11, 2001 attacks, has been proven. As a result, more people in the United States have started to criticize the war.

REACHING OUT: A U.S. soldier plays with children at a Baghdad park.

Iraqis, meanwhile, are living with the consequences. And some blame the U.S. for the violence and unrest in their nation. They want coalition troops to leave.

"These foreigners, they are ruining everything," says Sama Samir, an 11-year-old Iraqi girl. "I want to be safe." But others, including 14-year-old Said Fadhil, feel safer with the troops nearby.

After U.S. President Bush declared an official end to the war on May 1, 2003, unrest in Iraq grew. Murders and robberies rose dramatically. Thieves looted schools, stores, hospitals, and museums. "After Saddam was toppled, everything was a mess," says 12-year-old Mohammed Akbar. "Now, there are criminals in our neighborhood."

Gangs kidnap people, including children, off the streets and hold them for ransom. Cluster bomblets—tiny bombs that were dropped by U.S. warplanes during the war and look like colorful toys—explode when kids try to play with them.

CHILDREN AT RISK

For Iraqi kids, there are other dangers as well. Hundreds of young people have been killed in the crossfire between U.S.-led forces and rebels and militias that oppose the U.S. presence in Iraq. Other young people have been recruited to fight for the rebels. Because of such dangers, many parents have kept their children out of school.

Elaf Rami, 11, describes the dilemma that many young Iraqis face. "I'm afraid, but I want to go to school," she says, smiling shyly. "I want to study."

A NEW GOVERNMENT

In June 2004, U.S. officials handed over power to a temporary Iraqi government. Iraq's new prime minister, Ayad Allawi, immediately called for a crackdown on crime.

In many areas of Iraq, inci-dents of robbery and kidnapping began to drop, and people started going out after dark again. Ice cream stores were crowded with families.

But in Najaf, a city sacred to Shiites, the violence continued. The powerful Shiite leader Moktada al-Sadr, who wants the U.S. out of Iraq, encouraged his militia fighters to attack U.S. forces. And once again, violence spread to Baghdad and other areas.

The temporary government is scheduled to hold elections in 2005. If Allawi can make the country stable by then, Iraqis will have their first-ever democratic elections. But many people fear that continued violence will pre-vent elections from taking place.

GUNMEN: Militia fighters loyal to Shiite leader Moktada al-Sadr took to the streets in August 2004 to combat U.S. troops in Najaf.

JOINING FORCES: Soldiers in the new Iraqi army support U.S. troops during a battle with insurgents.

Who's Fighting Whom?
In Iraq, the conflict has gotten very complicated.

SEPT 2004—The war began as an invasion by U.S.-led forces. But the conflict has become increasingly complicated. Insurgents are launching attacks against the coalition troops. In addition, fierce fighting among Iraqi religious and ethnic groups has broken out.

Here's a look at who's fighting—and why.

COALITION FORCES: A U.S.-led coalition of 300,000 troops invaded Iraq in 2003. Most of the troops engaged in combat were American or British.

IRAQI ARMY: During the invasion, coalition forces fought Iraqi soldiers. But after a new Iraqi government was installed, Iraqi and U.S. troops joined forces. Together they battle various insurgent groups.

MILITIAS: In Iraq, there are two main Islamic sects: Sunnis and Shiites. Some leaders of groups within those sects command their own militias. These militias fight each other and also U.S. and Iraqi troops. This sectarian conflict has caused many civilian deaths.

INSURGENTS: These are rebel groups that oppose the U.S.-led coalition's occupation of Iraq. Most also oppose the new Iraqi government. Some are terrorists who have come from other countries to fight in Iraq. Their weapons include home-made bombs called IEDs (improvised explosive devices) or roadside bombs. These deadly devices are usually placed on roads and are triggered by passing vehicles or pedestrians.

ONE VOTE: An Iraqi woman casts her ballot on October 15.

A VOTE FOR DEMOCRACY

Iraqis vote on a new constitution.

The ballots have been counted, and the people of Iraq have a new constitution. On October 15, 2005, more than three-quarters of Iraqi voters chose to make the constitution the law of their nation.

The constitution requires the government to hold elections for a leader every four years, and it grants significant power to local governments. The constitution will also allow Iraqis to elect their first full-time parliament—a lawmaking body like the U.S. Congress—since Saddam Hussein ruled the country.

The approval of the constitution is a big step toward democracy. Elections for the new parliament will be held on December 15. The constitution will take effect after that election.

"It's a landmark day in the history of Iraq," said White House spokesman Scott McClellan.

REACTIONS TO THE VOTE

Of the three major ethnic groups in Iraq, most Shiites and Kurds voted for the constitution, while the Sunnis voted against it.

Critics of the new constitution fear that it will worsen the divide between Sunnis and the rest of Iraq's people. Saddam Hussein was a Sunni, and he awarded power to many Sunnis. With Hussein gone, Sunnis have lost

MEANWHILE: On October 19, 2005, Saddam Hussein went on trial for crimes against his people. He faces the death penalty.

much of their power. Now they fear that Shiites and Kurds will dominate the new government.

IRAQIS CHOOSE LEADERS

There's a huge turnout as voters pick new leaders.

On December 15, 2005, Iraqis chose a new government. About 70 percent of eligible voters participated in the historic vote. Mobbed polling places were largely free of violence.

Said current prime minister

BIG TURNOUT: About 70% of eligible voters went to the polls. Here, women go through a security checkpoint before voting.

Ibrahim al-Jaafari, "The real triumph is that people [have] chosen voting over bombs."

Iraqi and U.S. officials were pleased that many Sunnis voted. Sunnis are a minority in Iraq. But they held most of the power under Saddam Hussein.

Most Iraqis picked their new leaders on a strict religious or ethnic basis. Some observers say that this could indicate a permanent split among Shiite, Sunni, and Kurdish groups. No one knows whether Sunnis will peacefully accept a minority voice in the government.

45

SAYING GOOD-BYE: Sergeant Robert Beamon hugs his daughter Ashli.

GOOD-BYE AGAIN

As the war continues, many soldiers have to return to Iraq.

Brittney Espinal received a great surprise for her high school graduation in June 2006. Her father, Sergeant Major Louis Espinal of the U.S. Marine Corps, returned home from Iraq for a two-week visit.

"I got home from school. It was about three days before graduation," says the California teen. "It was a complete surprise."

Like many soldiers serving overseas, Brittney's father has had repeated deployments to Iraq. That means he's had to serve there many times. Brittney says it's always hard to say goodbye.

"People say it gets easier each time, but for me it doesn't," she says.

PULLING TOGETHER

Brittney lives with her mother and two sisters. "We're definitely more there to help my mom," Brittney says. She helps her mom with her little sister, who misses their dad a lot.

Although Brittney has friends and teachers to talk to, she is sometimes frustrated by her peers' lack of awareness about the war in Iraq. She has met teens who don't even realize the war is still going on.

To young people, Brittney says, "Always take advantage of having your parents there, of all the little moments. And keep educated about what's going on outside of the United States. So many times we [focus on] just what's happening here."

SOLDIER DAD: Brittney Espinal poses with her father.

MORE BOOTS ON THE GROUND

Will these girls' stepdad have to go back?

Courtney and Meghan Rinnert of Tracy, California, are among many kids in U.S. military families who are paying close attention to what is happening in Iraq. Their stepfather, Robert McKim, is in the Army Reserves and has already served a 15-month tour of duty in Iraq.

Courtney and Meghan are preparing for the possibility that their stepdad may be sent to Iraq again. "It's really hard for us," Meghan says. "We miss him a lot whenever he's gone."

In January 2007, U.S. President George W. Bush announced that he is sending more than 20,000 additional troops to Iraq. They'll aid in the effort to stabilize a country that many say is spinning out of control.

The U.S. currently has 132,000 troops in Iraq. The president says additional troops are needed to help the new Iraqi government gain control of the country.

TOGETHER: Robert McKim and his family. About 115,000 U.S. kids have parents serving in Iraq or Afghanistan.

47

LIVING IN FEAR

by James Palmer in Baghdad

Each day, Iraqi teens face violence, fear, and uncertainty.

KEEP AWAY: A young man warns people to stay clear of a car bomb explosion.

LOST FRIENDS: In 2007, Iraqi students carry a coffin and hold photographs of classmates killed in a car bomb attack the previous year.

Murthatha Emad, 13, lives along the banks of the Tigris River in Baghdad, the capital of Iraq. In July 2007, Murthatha was buying a hamburger from a neighborhood street vendor. Suddenly, an explosion tore through the crowded area, and more than 100 people were killed.

The blast was so powerful that it threw Murthatha to the ground and knocked him unconscious. When he awoke in the hospital days later, he had no memory of the attack. Twenty-three pieces of shrapnel (metal fragments) were lodged in his body.

"My family feared I was killed because they found me buried under a dead body," Murthatha said.

Life has become increasingly difficult for children in Baghdad. Just getting to school can be life-threatening. Insurgents routinely attack areas protected by Iraqi and U.S. security forces. Rival militias fight for control of neighborhoods. Armed criminal gangs roam the streets seeking victims to kidnap for ransom. At any moment, anyone can get caught in the crossfire.

Although he survived the attack, Murthatha is physically and psychologically scarred. "Now I'm afraid to leave my house," he said. "I don't want to return to school."

AMONG THE DISPLACED

No one knows exactly how many Iraqi civilians have been killed

49

INJURED: Murthatha Emad (left) was wounded when a bomb exploded in his neighborhood.

DISPLACED: After Marwan Kareem saw a man being murdered outside his school, his family moved.

FEARFUL: Rand Qusai says she wears modest clothes in public to avoid becoming a "target of the insurgents."

since the war began. Estimates range from 100,000 to more than 200,000. Today, most Iraqis believe that their government and security forces are incapable of protecting them. Many reluctantly say that the U.S. military must remain in the country to contain ongoing violence.

As the bloodshed continues, more and more Iraqis are being forced from their homes. Last summer, insurgent attacks forced Marwan Kareem, 15, and his family to flee from their home in the dangerous Diyala Province. Before that, Marwan witnessed the murder of a man outside his school. "I couldn't sleep for weeks after I saw the shooting," Marwan said. "I stopped going to school, and I was too afraid to leave my home."

PRISONERS IN THEIR HOMES

Life can be especially difficult for girls. In some areas, Muslim extremists prevent girls from attending school and force them to dress modestly in headscarves and *abayas*—loose-fitting robes.

"I would prefer to let my hair down and wear jeans and short-sleeved blouses," said 15-year-old Rand Qusai. "But I fear becoming a target of the insurgents or militias."

Mariam Farhad, 14, said that threats of violence have forced the closing of her all-girls' school in Baghdad several times. A blast near the school last June disrupted final exams. "The explosion shattered the windows," Mariam said, "and knocked the papers off our desks."

STAY OR LEAVE?

Many Iraqis feel that they have no choice except to leave their country. The UN estimates that more than two million people have left Iraq since the war began. About another two million people have been displaced within the country.

Mohammed Halam, 14, said that many of his friends have left for France, Jordan, Oman, or the United Arab Emirates. He keeps in touch with them by e-mail.

Mohammed's family is now trying to decide whether to remain in Iraq. "We're torn between staying here amid the violence and leaving our home to start a new life in a new country," Mohammed said. "Either way, it's going to be very difficult."

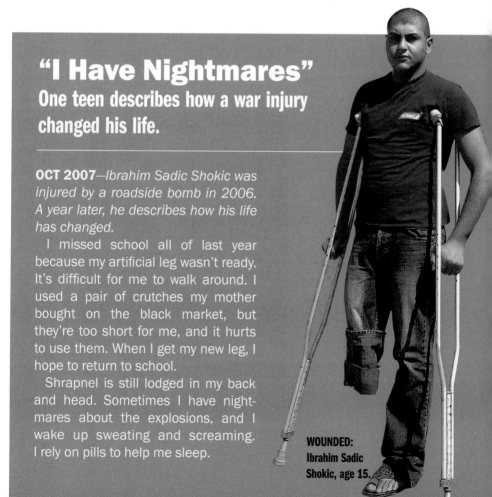

"I Have Nightmares"
One teen describes how a war injury changed his life.

OCT 2007—*Ibrahim Sadic Shokic was injured by a roadside bomb in 2006. A year later, he describes how his life has changed.*

I missed school all of last year because my artificial leg wasn't ready. It's difficult for me to walk around. I used a pair of crutches my mother bought on the black market, but they're too short for me, and it hurts to use them. When I get my new leg, I hope to return to school.

Shrapnel is still lodged in my back and head. Sometimes I have nightmares about the explosions, and I wake up sweating and screaming. I rely on pills to help me sleep.

WOUNDED:
Ibrahim Sadic
Shokic, age 15.

PROGRESS IN IRAQ?

Top U.S. general in Iraq says things are getting better.

We're making progress. That's according to U.S. General David H. Petraeus, commander of the coalition forces in Iraq. Last month, in September 2007, Petraeus appeared before the U.S. Congress to report on this year's "surge," during which 30,000 additional troops were sent to Iraq.

Petraeus said that the surge has helped U.S. and Iraqi forces to reduce violence and improve security in some of the most dangerous areas. The general also made a case against withdrawing troops too soon. That would endanger the progress that's been made so far. "A premature drawdown of our forces would likely have devastating consequences," he said.

Many politicians fear that the U.S. forces are stuck in the middle of a civil war between rival Sunni and Shiite groups, with no end in sight. And some lawmakers challenged the general's account of progress. "The surge has failed," said Representative Robert Wexler, pointing to a report that said war-related deaths have doubled in Iraq in 2007.

About 155,000 soldiers are now based in Iraq. Petraeus recommended that 30,000 of them leave by next July. But he would not set a timetable for further withdrawals.

PROGRESS REPORT: General Petraeus testified before the U.S. Congress in September 2007.

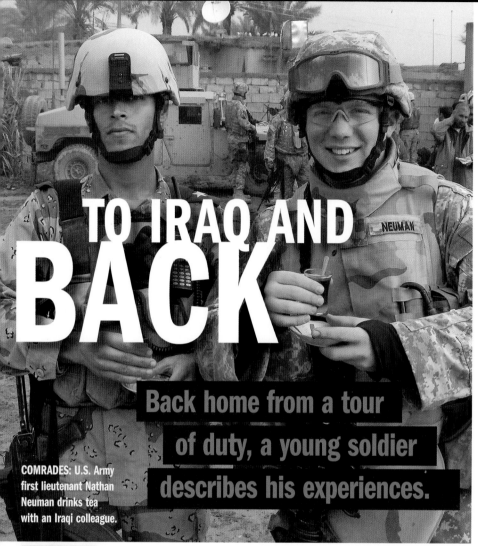

TO IRAQ AND BACK

Back home from a tour of duty, a young soldier describes his experiences.

COMRADES: U.S. Army first lieutenant Nathan Neuman drinks tea with an Iraqi colleague.

March 19, 2008, was the fifth anniversary of the start of the war in Iraq. About 155,000 brave U.S. military personnel continue to risk their lives there. Until recently, U.S. Army first lieutenant Nathan Neuman, 24, was one of them.

Nate, as his friends call him, says that besides the danger, the biggest personal challenge about being in Iraq was "separation from friends and family."

For now, Nate is back home with his loved ones in Buffalo, New York. He joined the army at age 18 and then earned a college

BUDDIES: Nate hangs out with his Iraqi friends at an army base.

full readiness, you're in full protective gear and equipment," Nate says. "You could get blown up during a short drive."

HIDDEN DANGERS

"You aren't fighting an organized government or military," Nate explains. "You're fighting insurgents, who do not wear a uniform and fade into civilian crowds when they don't want to fight anymore."

This kind of warfare is frustrating for both Americans and Iraqis because it doesn't distinguish between combatants and civilians.

"You don't know who you're fighting," Nate says. "A guy puts a bomb on the side of the road and hides in a ditch 150 meters away. The bomb goes off, he walks away, and you never knew what hit you. You don't know who to shoot at. All you see are three Iraqi civilians standing nearby, but they're innocent. They're just as scared and shocked as you are."

degree. In spring 2006, after graduation and training, he was sent to Iraq for a one-year tour of duty.

Nate's job was to help the Iraqi government, the U.S. military, and private contractors work together to build or rebuild roads and other infrastructure. His unit also provided humanitarian aid.

Nate lived with 3,000 other U.S. military and Iraqi personnel on a one-square-mile base near the city of Baqubah. He says life on base was like "being on call 24/7." Some days started as early as 5:00 A.M. with a meeting to discuss the day's missions.

Because of security issues, even the simple task of fixing a power line could take all day and present danger. "Anytime you leave the [base], it's considered a combat situation, which means you're on

COMMON BOND

According to Nate, life hasn't been easy for the people of Iraq. "They really have suffered for a very long time, starting with the war against

Iran in the 1980s, followed by the Persian Gulf war, followed by . . . another war and insurgency. They think they're cursed," he says.

In spite of their differences, Nate found ways to connect with his Iraqi colleagues, especially his interpreter, Ali. Now they stay in touch by e-mail. "It's amazing how all humanity is the same to an extent—the will to do good, general expressions in body language, subtle emotions," he says. "You have to look for it, but you can have a common bond with anybody."

Even though Nate was happy to go home, leaving Iraq was bittersweet. "You develop friendships with the people you're trying to help, and it's difficult to walk away."

Will Nate have to go back to Iraq? "We are such a strained military that you have soldiers going back for second and third tours," Nate says. "Everybody goes back."

Should U.S. Troops Leave Iraq?
Here are two perspectives on this debate.

Yes: Troops Out Now

"I think [U.S. troops] should withdraw immediately," said Sara Ramsey, a ninth-grader who lives in Essex, Missouri. "So many of our men and women are fighting and losing their lives for a battle that we can't win."

Justin Brock, 14, thinks so, too. He believes that the United States is sending the wrong message by keeping troops in Iraq. "I don't want Iraq to think we're trying to take over and create a colony for ourselves," said the ninth-grader from Jackson, Michigan. "I just want the troops home!"

No: Not Yet

"We should keep the troops there for a while to get the job done, no matter what the price," says Marissa Maggio, a seventh-grader from Lodi, California. She went on: "From interviews I've read, the soldiers in Iraq believe in the cause and are anxious to finish the job. They are seeing the benefits."

Kay-Lea Wilde agrees. The 13-year-old thinks that an immediate withdrawal would make a bad situation worse. "If we withdrew immediately," she said, "then [Iraqis] would have more problems, and [we would be no closer to achieving] peace."

AN UNCLEAR FUTURE: An Iraqi boy looks through the broken window of a minibus hit by a roadside bomb. What does the future hold for him and for others affected by the war?

TIMELINE

1980: A year after becoming president, Saddam Hussein starts a war with Iran. The war lasts eight years. More than a million people die.

1990: Iraqi troops invade the neighboring country of Kuwait and seize control of its oil fields.

1991: The U.S. and its allies launch a counter-attack called Operation Desert Storm. They free Kuwait, but Saddam Hussein stays in power. Iraq is ordered to disarm and allow UN weapons inspectors into the country.

1998: UN inspectors say that Iraq is blocking their work. They leave. The U.S. and Great Britain bomb suspected Iraqi weapons sites.

2002: The UN orders Iraq to allow inspectors back in—or face severe consequences. Hussein complies.

2003: President Bush says that Iraq has weapons of mass destruction (WMDs). In March, U.S.-led forces begin Operation Iraqi Freedom.

2003: Hussein is driven out of power. On May 1, President Bush announces an end to major hostilities. But the fighting continues. In December, Hussein is captured.

2005: Saddam Hussein goes on trial. Iraqis approve a constitution and elect a new government.

2006: Violence among rival groups in Iraq gets worse. Saddam Hussein is executed.

2007: 30,000 more U.S. troops are sent to Iraq to support the 132,000 troops already there.

2008: March 19 marks the fifth anniversary of the start of the war. Fighting continues, but security for Iraqi citizens is said to be improving. The World Health Organization estimates that 150,000 Iraqis have died as a result of the war.

2009: A new U.S. presidential administration takes over; Iraq is a top item on the agenda.

MARCH 2003: The war began with the bombing of Baghdad.

Resources

Looking for more information? Here are some resources you don't want to miss.

WEBSITES

World Factbook: Iraq
https://www.cia.gov/library/
publications/the-world-factbook/
geos/iz.html

For a brief overview of Iraq, check out this profile from the CIA.

**National Geographic
Hot Spot: Iraq**
http://www.nationalgeographic.
com/iraq

Explore this site to find maps, articles, and a wealth of information about Iraq and the Middle East.

Youth Radio: War and Iraq
http://www.youthradio.org/
politics/iraqindex.shtml

Find out what other young people have to say about the situation in Iraq. Hear reports from the front lines.

International Committee of the Red Cross: The ICRC in Iraq
http://www.icrc.org/web/
eng/siteeng0.nsf/htmlall/
iraq?opendocument&link=home

Stay up to date on the Red Cross's humanitarian efforts in Iraq.

University of Southern California Glossary of Islamic Terms and Concepts
http://cwis.usc.edu/dept/MSA/reference/glossary.html

If you want to learn more about the Muslim faith, this glossary is a fantastic reference tool. You'll find definitions of important terms, prayers, people, traditions, and concepts.

United Nations Weapons of Mass Destruction Branch of the UN Office for Disarmament Affairs
http://disarmament.un.org/WMD

This site provides information about the UN's worldwide efforts to contain or destroy devastating nuclear, chemical, and biological weapons.

BOOKS

Augustin, Byron and Jake Kubena. *Iraq* (Enchantment of the World, Second Series). Danbury, Conn.: Children's Press, 2006.

Balaghi, Shiva. *Saddam Hussein: A Biography* (Greenwood Biographies). Westport, Conn.: Greenwood Press, 2005.

Carlisle, Rodney P. and John Stewart Bowman. *Iraq War* (America at War). New York: Facts on File, 2004.

Samuels, Charlie. *Iraq* (National Geographic Countries of the World). Washington, D.C.: National Geographic Children's Books, 2007.

Williams, Julie. *Islam: Understanding the History, Beliefs, and Culture* (Issues in Focus Today). Berkeley Heights, N.J.: Enslow Publishers, 2008.

Dictionary

A

Al Qaeda (ahl KYE-duh) *noun* an international network of terrorists inspired by Osama bin Laden, a Sunni Muslim from Saudi Arabia

allies (AL-ize) *noun* two or more countries working together for a common cause

ambushes (AM-bush-ez) *noun* surprise attacks from hidden locations

B

biological weapons (bye-uh-LAWJ-ih-kuhl WEH-puhnz) *noun* weapons that spread viruses or bacteria and cause deadly diseases

C

chemical weapons (KEM-ih-kuhl WEH-puhnz) *noun* weapons that release poisonous gases or other toxic substances

civilians (sih-VIHL-yenz) *noun* people not on active duty in a military or police force; innocent bystanders

coalition (koh-uh-LISH-uhn) *noun* a group of nations or organizations that cooperate for a certain purpose on a temporary basis

D

deployments (dih-PLOY-mentz) *noun* periods of wartime service by soldiers

dictator (DIHK-tay-tehr) *noun* a leader who rules with absolute power, and who uses intimidation or force to maintain control

E

exile (EGG-zyle) *noun* a period of forced absence from one's home or country

extremists (ex-TREEM-ihsts) *noun* people with radical beliefs who are willing to use violence against those who oppose them

G

Green Zone (green zohn) *noun* a four-square-mile area in central Baghdad that houses coalition forces and other international interests; also called the International Zone

H

humanitarian aid (hew-MAN-ih-TARE-ee-uhn AYD) *noun* help for people who lack basic needs, such as food, water, and shelter

I

insurgents (in-SURJ-entz) *noun* people who rebel against the established government or authority

Islam (iss-LAHM) *noun* a religion based on the teachings of Muhammad. Its followers are called Muslims. They believe that Allah is God, and that Muhammad is Allah's prophet. The Islamic holy book is the Koran.

K

Kurds (kihrdz) *noun* members of an ethnic group whose population is spread over parts of Turkey, Iraq, Iran, Syria, and Armenia

M

Muslims (MUHZ-luhmz) *noun* people who follow the religion of Islam

R

refugees (REF-yoo-jeez) *noun* people who flee their homelands because of mistreatment or danger

regime (reh-ZHEEM) *noun* a government currently in power

S

sects (sektz) *noun* groups within a broader religious faith

Shiites (SHEE-ytes) *noun* members of the smaller of the two great sects of Muslims

Sunnis (SOON-eez) *noun* members of the larger of the two great sects of Muslims

T

terrorists (TEHR-uh-ristz) *noun* people who use violence against civilians as a political tool

W

weapons of mass destruction (WEH-puhnz uhv MASS dih-STRUK-shuhn) *noun* biological, chemical, or nuclear weapons that can kill large numbers of people or cause great damage

Index

About This Book

The articles in this book were adapted from pieces that appeared originally in five Scholastic magazines. Sources include the following:

2002–2003: THE WAR BEGINS

Junior Scholastic: Volume 105, issue 4/5, October 18–25, 2002; Volume 105, issue 14, March 14, 2003; Volume 105, issue 16, April 11, 2003; Volume 105, issue 17, April 25, 2003; Volume 105, issue 18, May 9, 2003; Volume 106, issue 1, September 1, 2003

Scholastic News 5/6: Volume 71, issue 4, September 27, 2002; Volume 71, issue 22, April 4, 2003; Volume 71, issue 23, April 11, 2003; Volume 71, issue 24, April 25, 2003; Volume 71, issue 25, May 2, 2003; Volume 72, issue 6, October 20, 2003

Scholastic News Online: March 19, 2003, October 20, 2003; December 15, 2003

Scholastic Action Magazine: Volume 27, issue 1, September 1, 2003

2004 AND BEYOND: NO END IN SIGHT

Junior Scholastic: Volume 106, issue 10, January 5, 2004; Volume 107, issue 2, September 20, 2004; Volume 108, issue 7, November 14, 2005; Volume 108, issue 11, January 23, 2006; Volume 108, issue 12, February 6, 2006; Volume 109, issue 11, January 22, 2007; Volume 110, issue 4, October 15, 2007; Volume 110, issue 7, November 12, 2007

Scholastic News 5/6: Volume 75, issue 15, February 12, 2007

Scholastic News Online: February 2004; October 27, 2005

Scholastic Scope Magazine: Volume 52, issue 14, March 8, 2004; Volume 55, issue 5, October 30, 2006; Volume 56, issue 11, February 4, 2008

CONTENT CONSULTANT: Roger Owen, Harvard University